Contents

M000003872

A Handbook for Badass Spiritual Warriors

ELEVEN POWERFUL TOOLS
TO IGNITE YOUR SPIRITUAL
CONNECTION

CORINNE LEBRUN M.S.

First Printing: 2019
ISBN 978-1-7984-1844-4
www.wilddivinebliss.org

Dedication

This book is dedicated to all of the spiritual seekers who sometimes struggle to maintain their connection to the divine and may feel that they need a little help to get back on the path. Have faith and know this: the path will meet you as soon as you set your eyes on it again.

ACKNOWLEDGMENTS

MY DEEPEST GRATITUDE to my spiritual badass partner, Jason Hand, who holds me accountable to my dreams. I also want to thank the other key badass spiritual warriors in my life who have inspired this piece of work: Janet Westrup, Kyle Wannigman, and Maire-Claire Voorhees. I give you my heartfelt appreciation for your never-ending support in listening to my spiritual musings and insights, and for sharing the journey. I also want to thank Philippe Menos and J.J. Sample for their guidance in bringing this work of the heart to life.

FOREWORD

AN INDIVIDUAL WHO is called upon to live a spiritual life in the modern world will be faced with many challenges. This journey—which is not for the timid or the avoidant—is the beginning of the hero's journey, the call to doing more than just falling into the habit of life. It requires the courage to not only face life head-on but to face one's hidden assumptions by delving into and dispelling one's deepest fears. This journey is rewarded with magic, fulfillment, and a wonder greater than the heart can ever imagine. But hold tight because the tides of the journey will bring waves of rebirth and expansion into the ocean of life. Learning the tools to stay afloat, while withstanding the turbulent waters, requires vigilance, patience, self-acceptance, and love.

I offer this handbook to give you shortcuts to revive or maintain your spiritual connection. Of course, its powerful tools can be used to build on your journey as well. The methods described in this guide have been gleaned from the most time-proven spiritual practices, as well as from powerful personal insights and scientific inquiry.

CHAPTER ONE

The Badass Spiritual Warrior

I ALWAYS FANCIED myself a warrior of sorts. While other girls were playing with dolls and painting their nails, I was imagining myself as a great wizard with magical powers. I would fight rouge tesseract bursts from other dimensions and keep the earth safe. I also enjoyed athletic challenges, especially gymnastics, and developed the grit required to thrive in karate classes. Since I was a child, I felt a deep calling to connect with the divine and the mystical, and was honestly more than a little irritated to learn that the path was going to require deep introspection before its secrets would be revealed to me. My mentor would always say that you can't jump ahead spiritually —I first had to do the work appropriate to my level of consciousness in order to evolve. Little did I know then, that he was training me to embody the tools of a spiritual warrior, the tools a badass needs to be part of the world and to dance in it.

If you live in this modern world and have any spiritual inclination, inevitably you will be forced to become a spiritual warrior or live with a constant nagging that something in your life is off balance. Spiritual warriors have the ability to meet the challenges of everyday life, as well as the courage to face the challenges of introspection and personal growth. A spiritual warrior's cause is spiritual connection and enlightenment. Their nemesis lies in being trapped by their own psychic shadows and by their own destructive habits.

Being a Badass Spiritual Warrior means you ***entirely*** take control of your life and, ironically, completely surrender to the divine. What a tightrope! There is no room for being a victim of any kind, because you either have to learn the lesson or do it again.

A badass is not controlled by the whims of other people's energies, by solar flares, electromagnetic frequencies (EMF'S), nor by astrological influences. They seek out the knowledge and tools they need to navigate any situation and *implement* them. They take action! Being a badass is having ninjalike skills to move in and out of daily life and remain content, fluid like water, while not being afraid to kick down the doors of perception. They fully participate in life and are a power of example through action. It is a great ideal to hold.

I have learned that Badass Spiritual Warriors aren't made overnight. They have to learn about their personal strengths and weaknesses, face many inner demons and know *how and when to ask for help*. And that takes learning about your own limitations and trusting your instincts. They know **how** to roll when they fall down in life and then get back up. They don't take no for an answer when it comes to connecting with the divine and are deeply compelled to do the work required to maintain that. They learn to trust there is a time for action, and don't judge themselves when it is a time of non-action or simply healing.

My favorite contemporary spiritual warriors who are in the public eye are Russel Brand, Jim Carrey, Amma and Oprah Winfrey. Exceptional warriors from the past who I particularly admire are Jesus, Mother Theresa, Yogi Bhajan, and Mahatma Gandhi. Each of these people has managed to live as active participants in the world, overcome extraordinary challenges and then create positive social change and spiritual awareness. They are not concerned with other people's opinions and stand for a greater spiritual truth.

Other types of badass spiritual warriors (who aren't afraid to get their hands dirty) are nurses, doctors, treatment center therapists, homeless shelter volunteers, school teachers, and relief workers. Faced with the unpredictable, these badass spiritual warriors navigate incredibly challenging circumstances using their wisdom and skillsets with grace and perseverance. They also understand the importance of self-care to stay aligned and grounded.

CHAPTER TWO

The Waves of Spiritual Growth

MAINTAINING ONE'S SPIRITUAL connection on a day-to-day basis can be very challenging, even for the most adept yogis. Sometimes people have come to me, ashamed that they have lost their magical union. This is especially true for people who have—at one time or another—experienced a life-changing Kundalini Awakening or paradigm-shattering spiritual experience. It seems inexplicable and disconcerting to go from a space of unshakable faith and extrasensory connection perception to feeling like a "regular human" again. In fact, knowing what one has lost –an extraordinary divine connection— makes the loss feel unbearable. Falling off the ladder of mystical love is indeed a dark night of the soul.

I have experienced this from time to time as well. I officially began my spiritual journey with a mentor when I was 17 years old. Since then, I have been through cycles of incredible expansion, supersensory perception, and mystic bliss, only to find myself back at the feet of the world, humbled that I am only human. The first time a sense of spiritual disconnection crept in, I thought I had done something wrong. I felt a deep sadness that I had somehow failed God and fell off my spiritual path. But what finally set my heart at ease was the realization that all aspects of life have cycles, even spiritual connection. This experience can result from waves of karmic nodes being activated, planetary influences, or simply angels lovingly standing in our way. A downward cycle is not inherently wrong or a sign of failure. We can consider ourselves blessed that, even in those times, our soul will whisper in our ear and nag us to find a sense of fulfillment and connection again.

For most people, staying spiritually connected in a stressful modern world doesn't happen naturally. I have found it *incredibly challenging* to maintain the expansive state of consciousness that I've felt during peak spiritual experiences. They usually contract as a result of getting emotionally triggered by some type of unresolved personal traumas or by being blindsided by events I hadn't anticipated. These triggers include hiccups in personal relationships, physical injuries, unexpected job losses, and even sometimes working too hard and not allowing time for enough self-care.

Whatever the cause, I have learned that we are only human. The quest to maintain a spiritual connection while being a badass modern-day yogi living in society (instead of a quiet monastery), is truly something we can be proud of. We have stamina, grit, a longing to channel the divine, and a drive to evolve. By joining efforts, we elevate each other.

But staying elevated isn't a constant. The spiritual connection can come in waves and cycles. This knowledge motivates me to share with others who are on the journey, compare notes, learn from various spiritual teachers, and observe in my own experience that the ebbs and flows of spiritual connection are only natural.

In those times when we are at a low and wonder, "Where are my synchronicities?" "Where is the magic I once felt?" it can truly feel like darkness. During those times, I have felt as though I was a mere shadow of my former, magical self. It was almost as though there was a shroud of forgetfulness hanging over me, and no matter how hard I tried to get back to feeling connected, my higher state of consciousness seemingly had forgotten itself. But with patience and a myriad of helping hands —both of this world and not of this world— I have always been able to find my way back to feeling spiritually connected, with a clear and vibrant channel to the divine.

Over time, I took notes and developed a handy list of action items to facilitate getting back on track.

When I feel like I can barely remember what it is I'm supposed to do to feel connected again, I go back to this powerful list, which initially consisted of notes on my bulletin board or thoughts tucked away in one of my journals. This list has been so incredibly helpful to me and others with whom I've shared it with, that I feel compelled to share it with more people by writing this book.

Generally speaking, to feel right with the world, I discovered that I have to do certain things every day. If I don't, I get that strange feeling of impending doom; *or* that somehow, I'm just not doing the things I'm *supposed* to be doing. But I found that some badass tenacity is what usually creates a breakthrough.

On many occasions, I have been challenged to find the time and energy to put a few of these tools in action. Yet, when I've made the time, and when I pay attention to what is happening in my inner world (as opposed to focusing only on the outer world), I've found that life goes more smoothly. I then feel like I am blessed to be in the flow of the Eternal *Tao*.

Those are the days when the world seems completely in sync. I see a pedestrian walking in step with the beat of the music on my car stereo, together with the rhythm of the nearby blinking traffic lights. A friend I'd been thinking about over the last week calls me and says something I heard in a dream the night before. All the street lights are green, and I arrive at my destination exactly on time, finding the only parking spot available. It's a magical experience, and you wonder if you are awake or having a very lucid dream.

Most of western society encourages an unbalanced and unhealthy focus on the outer world. It is very challenging to not become hypnotized by our culture, social media, and the fast pace of technological development. But if we spend a thousandth of the time on our inner worlds –that we spend dwelling about our outer worlds– then we will find that magic and mysticism actually exist *right here in this dimension*, and that the Self does *not* have to escape the world in any way to experience the joy and knowledge of Union.

CHAPTER THREE

Eleven Powerful Practices

THESE ELEVEN PRACTICES are tools I have referred back to over and over again. After many years of traveling down the road of a spiritual warrior, learning the tools to become even an occasional badass, I earned some pearls of wisdom. Eventually, I began to share my wisdom with other people on the path. I found that the items on this list seemed universal from other paths, and worked not only for me but helped people live the middle road without judgment.

Each of these tools is powerful by itself. They are most powerful when done daily. Personally, I find the most effective results occur when I dedicate at least

20 minutes to myself in the morning the moment I wake up and my feet hit the floor. On the most ideal days, I am able to combine prayer, Kundalini Yoga, meditation, a cold shower and positive visualization of how I would like my day to go. At the end of the day, I log my important experiences into my Spiritual Log Book and am able to give myself positive affirmation that everything is indeed unfolding with the highest evolution as long as I am giving it my best effort. All of this allows me to connect with my own wisdom and soul before the chatter in my mind has a chance to begin. All of these practices contribute to my "spiritual bank account."

There are days where I am limited to what morning practices I can do based on human events, such as emergencies, travelling, oversleeping, my son needing attention, or having that "oh crap" moment where I realize I have 15 minutes to get out of the house because of an appointment I forgot about. On those days, I remind myself to ask God-Source for help and do some intentional breathing. But I make a conscious effort to not let too many days like this stack up, or my spiritual bank account gets depleted and feels empty. I respond by feeling like I need extra time with myself and Spirit. Even a three-minute breath of fire meditation, based on the Kundalini Yoga tradition, always does wonders to synchronize my brain hemispheres and calm down my nervous system. In really tense situations, I'm not above hiding in the bathroom and doing a short breathing practice.

THE SPIRITUAL LOG BOOK

There is nothing like doing something physical to let your mind, body, and spirit know that you are committed to creating change in your life. Get a fresh journal that has a cover that inspires joy in you when you look at it. Be sure it contains only positive messages, or simply an inspiring image. Committing to getting this journal will let your conscious mind know that you mean business. Also, seeing this journal next on your night stand every day, will remind you to make your daily entries and serve as a way to "prime" your mind to be more aware of tracking very specific events that happen in both the outer world and the inner world. Having and using this book is a psychological tool that will help you overcome negative patterns that may be blocking you from maintaining your spiritual connection.

This brand-new journal is dedicated to honoring your spiritual connection. It is important that this is not combined with an old journal, or journaling that is meant for emotional release, processing or goal setting. This journal will be a special place that you will treat as a log book, rather than a journal that processes your thoughts or emotions. It will become as useful book of scientific inquiry, where you are the experiment. You will find yourself looking back in this book and remarking on how interconnected so many things are! But it takes time to see the patterns. Begin by trusting the forces that are guiding you and seeing the patterns will follow. With time and history, your rational mind will stop arguing with you.

You can choose to divide the Journal/Log Book into sections or create a key code in front of each entry.

Log in your dreams, synchronicities, unexpected gifts, sensations of energy, divine messages and interdimensional experiences *every day*. A useful technique is to close your eyes and go through your entire day, at the end of the day. Recall if there were any magical or psychic moments, synchronicities, or unexpected invitations that came your way. Additionally, if you can remember your dreams, either write them down in the morning and/or in the evening. You can continue to add categories to your list, but the point is to make this process a simple and fast logbook in which to make your entries each day.

KEY CODES:

S—*Synchronicities*

G—*Unexpected gifts*

I—*Interdimensional experiences/magical moments*

D—*Dreams*

E—*Sensations of Energy*

M—*Messages from meditations and prayers*

Here are some examples:

Synchronicity—You make a decision that you want to go to Hawaii for a vacation, and you have it on your vision board. That evening, you unexpectedly get invited to a friend's house for a party that has a Hawaiian theme. Your entry might look like:

> **S**—*Put Hawaii on vision board; Cathy's party was Hawaiian themed.*

Unexpected gifts—Once you start to look, you will begin to notice all of the unexpected gifts that the universe delivers. A gift might be in the form of discounts, found objects, free concert tickets, or an unexpected thank you. Keeping track of these gifts creates an opening for you to receive them and experience the joy they are meant to inspire. An entry can look something like this:

> **G**—*Laura gave me a gift bag of hand lotion from a conference she attended.*

Interdimensional experiences—This is the category where everything that seems out of the ordinary for a

Newtonian physics world (aside from synchronicities) gets placed. For example, things that belong in this category are experiences of telepathy; precognition; seeing chakra colors; time anomalies; miracle healings; telekinesis; and sensations of angels, ghosts, or spirit guides.

Here is an example of a few entries:

I—*Aura - Saw purple lights around Cindy's head.*

I—*Time Anomaly - I walked downtown which usually takes 30 minutes. I found I made it in 10 minutes and had double checked the time before I left. Even my friend Kenzie had called right before I left, and that was only ten minutes from my arrival time.*

I—*My intuition said to go to the Cat's Paw Coffee shop at 2:00. I found my friend Nancy there who really needed someone to talk to.*

Eventually, when you practice logging your experiences, you will find that this interdimensional experience category can be broken down even further. You may end up having separate sections for seeing auras, clairvoyance, and obtaining information from spirit guides.

Dreams—A category for your dreams at night. You can be as elaborate as you want, or just write down a few notes to help you remember the dream in the future. You may use a poignant dream for a deep dive into dream interpretation to find out what your subconscious or your inner guidance is telling you. Or you may find that some of your dreams are precognitive, and you can look back in your journal and enjoy your magical wisdom! An example of how simple your entry can be:

> **D**—*Fish were flying, and the rain turned into a waterfall on a house. Tabatha was there and gave me roses.*

Sensations of Energy—Sometimes people feel or sense energy as if they had an extra body around them that also can feel electromagnetic energy, and emotions and morphogenic fields. Everyone has this capacity, and it just takes practice to notice it and expand your capacity to take in information consciously from this "antenna" your body has. People who have gone through sudden Kundalini Awakenings sometimes find this capacity suddenly awakens and they feel a bit like a cat without its fur to protect it. Other people find that this capacity unfolds more gradually and is less jarring for the senses. I recall the first time I actually "saw" an energy field around a bird, and the first time I actually "felt" a crystal. When I felt the crystal if felt like a pressure against my whole extended energy body that was filled with dancing light particles. As time goes on, and you pay attention to these supersensory perceptions, this capacity grows.

One important thing to remember is ***not to attach meaning*** to any of your observations. It is when we assign a meaning based on emotional attachments that our interpretations may send us down a path of unnecessary hardship. It takes self-knowledge, time, and practice to understand the psychological dynamics unconsciously driving our emotions. Therefore, it is best to be an observer of energetic phenomena, and its meaning eventually becomes clear after watching the patterns, as well as learning tools used by credible sources.

Here are some examples of how to make entries about energy. If you don't feel them yet (I didn't for years), don't worry because it will come.

> **E**—*Felt there was a crystal in the room, only to find out it was hidden behind a big chair.*

> **E**—*Felt energy move through me, it felt like little molecules of peace moving through me.*

> **E**—*Felt like the area over my heart was buzzing.*

Messages—Learning to watch your interior world is just as important as watching the exterior world. I found that when I meditate, it is useful to take time after the meditation to ask for guidance. What works best for me is to visualize myself walking into a safe place, that is my inner sanctuary and sitting in a delightful garden or temple space that feels comfortable. While I am sitting in there, I ask a question and then ask for guidance. Most of the time I am given a symbol, a word, or some type of message. When I come out of the meditation, I write down the message and often find that later in the day the image will connect with something I had yet to experience. Tracking these types of messages is a great boost to our conscious mind, opening ourselves to understand and allow for interdimensional experiences to connect with our everyday world.

Here are some examples of how to log this:

M—*In my meditation a blue light came and gave me a purple rose. Later in the day someone randomly walked up to me and gave me a purple rose.*

M—*In my meditation I heard the word carpenter. Later that day I received a flyer about carpenters in my neighborhood.*

When you are doing your daily review, if you find that you have not experienced any of these things, then just write "nothing to report." This may go on for a few days or even a few weeks at a time, but know that the more you take time to listen and watch the universe and the universe inside you, the more these experiences will be revealed over time. Know, too, that it is totally normal to sometimes have a sprint of extraordinary synchronicities and times of deep connection to Spirit, and then hear absolutely nothing. Think of the quiet times as periods of integration, another wave in your journey. As long as your effort and sincerity remain constant, your pent-up energy will eventually reveal itself, releasing in you another massive wave of a blessed connection to the hidden dimensions of the universe.

"Turn it over" to a Higher Power

I often need to remind myself that there is a power that will guide me, far greater than my own intelligence and emotions. Most westerners have a conditioned inclination to muscle through things, through the sheer power of will. But when I remember there is an organizing force in the universe far more intelligent than me, I am reminded this is how to hack "the game." I think about the fact that this incredible intelligence has created the astounding mechanisms of our bodies. I wonder at the photo finish eyes of the owl butterfly's wings. I marvel at the fact that our physical world is held together only by the *vibration* of electrons, as there is mostly space between the small building blocks of matter. The intelligence required to compile a string of DNA and understand its language to create a unique life form, is far beyond any human capacity.

Once my faith is revived in a power greater than myself, I find a way to ask for help from God-Source. The idea of "turning things over" means to turn *all* of my problems, questions, frustrations, and victories over to the care of what I define as my Higher Power. When I get my ego out of the way and listen, solutions I had not considered present themselves.

Whatever you believe in —that is greater than your own mind; whatever you may call God, the Force, the Source, the Goddess, Buddha, Jesus, the Tao, or Mohammed— the label doesn't matter. Just call upon its wisdom and surrender, and let go the best you can. Even simply creating a dedicated place to pray or creating a daily ritual will help soothe your conscious and unconscious mind.

I find that connecting with others who believe in a power greater than themselves and listening to what they have to say truly elevates me and my thinking. This experience can also be derived by reading a passage from an inspirational book, attending spiritually-based groups, going to kirtan and listening to spiritually-based podcasts. All of these methods ignite my trust in a power greater than mine. When I seek positive input, beyond my own thoughts, my mind becomes open to new thoughts and deeds, grounded in an elevated perspective.

Remind yourself that everything is perfectly on schedule and is unfolding in life as it should be, that you are exactly where you are supposed to be. By accepting the moment *and* yourself in that moment, you are removing the struggle and empowering yourself. Trust that your higher power is leading you to a more fulfilling life and that all you have to do is start to pay attention to the messages you receive. If I feel like I'm faltering or need to renew my faith in a specific area, I pray for a sign. I don't usually need to pray for any longer than a few days.

HONOR YOUR BODY

One of the fastest ways to accelerate your spiritual growth is to honor your body. The first piece that most people overlook is the importance of getting enough sleep. Just getting enough sleep can lift people out of depression, relieve anxiety, and heal potentially fatal diseases. Find your own ideal amount of sleep by allowing yourself to go to bed early enough, so that you will wake up on your own without an alarm clock. Eventually, with some experimentation, you will find the ideal amount of time your body needs rest. For each person it is different and may vary over time. Some people consistently need 10 hours, and others only need 5. Don't judge yourself, just give your body what it needs.

Another more obvious area is to review your food habits. Are you eating enough, too much, what time are your meals, and is the content of your meals serving you? For example, if you tend to be hypoglycemic, eating sweets and going a long time between meals will leave you feeling jittery and overly emotional. If you are eating a donut for breakfast, your brain cells will feel sluggish. If you are in habits that you know are not serving your body or your mindset, commit to a discipline of balanced eating for one week, and you will be amazed at how easy it will be to have more balanced habits at the end of it.

What you eat will affect your mind, body, emotions, and your spiritual state of wellbeing. Finding what your individual body needs to run optimally, may be different than what you have believed in the past. It is important to listen to your own body's intuition rather than what might be healthy for someone else. To figure out what is going to work best for you personally, ask yourself how you feel after you consume various foods. How much energy do you have, and what is the quality of your life force. Are you feeling vital or dull and sluggish?

There are many different combinations of genetic predispositions that will determine how food is metabolized by your unique body. To me, being spiritual simply means consciously taking the middle road, nothing in excess, and honoring all life especially if you consume it for your own energy. There are countless options for diets; pescatarian, vegetarian, vegan, omnivores, macrobiotic, paleo centric, etc. I remember when I stopped being a vegetarian after seven years and went back to being an omnivore. I felt better and was far more easily able to be present in the world, and with my spiritual path. This is what worked best for my genetic makeup and what my energy body needs to thrive. It is not the same for everyone. Learning to listen to your intuition about what your body needs takes some practice. But honoring its needs is essential to having a firm foundation in staying present and feeling a sense of inner strength.

Exercise of some type is also necessary to keep your body functioning in its optimal form. If you are in good health, without injuries, then keeping a warrior's body will be the ideal. Any type of strenuous exercise will raise your energy levels and expand your aura. I found that practices like Kundalini Yoga, Marshall Arts, Tai Chi help to strengthen the energy in my third chakra (aside with their numerous other spiritual benefits) *which is essential to being energetically stable and not taking on other people's energy.* These practices also increase your auric field, which can actually be measured. This is one of the most important tools a spiritual badass warrior will have. You will be able to go anywhere and meet the energy with your energy field., rather than having the energy meet you. You will feel centered emotionally and not let other people's energy affect you. You will still feel the energy and be able to use it for your own intuition, but you will not be controlled by it. And with practice, you will know when you need to retreat and re-charge. Generally, any type of physical activity that will elevate your heart rate will have energetic benefits and will stimulate your lymphatic system which will keep your body healthy, and leave your mind feeling optimized.

Finally, I will mention the cold shower. Using cold showers in the morning is a tool used by Badass

Yogis in many traditions. For example, the ancient Greeks, Romans, Russians, Japanese practitioner of Shinto, Taoists all practiced cold showers. The first time I heard about doing cold showers was while I was doing the Kundalini Yoga Teacher training. I thought, "Hell no, I'm not going to put my skinny ass into a cold shower. I'll freeze! That can't be good for me!" It took a few years to warm up to the concept. This was reinforced when I met my partner, who was already doing cold showers because he was following the recommendations of Vim Hof, who is a Dutch extreme athlete. People who have gone through the Vim Hof training seem to be superhuman. They can swim through ice lakes and melt snow with their bodies. So, I became even more curious about the recommendation the Yogi's had already made.

I found studies that show cold showers have an enormous amount of health benefits. Just some of the benefits are: to improve immunity and circulation, stimulate brown fat weight loss, speed up muscle recovery, ease stress, relieve depression, increase testosterone, and balance the glands. That was hard for me to argue with. So I finally decided to try it. I find the initial shock wakes me up and gets my brain ready for the day, far better than my usual cup of coffee.

The practice of taking regular cold showers is a spiritual discipline. It is the first action of the day that you can use to conquer your smaller self. It is a way of hacking your brain into doing the difficult things that are required to get you to break through patterns and habits that do not serve you. When you are consistently doing this for yourself in one area of your life, then it becomes easier to do this in other areas of your life. Your brain gets used to conquering old ideas, and it becomes less scary to evolve. The resistance that can be built up as a result of bad habit no longer has as much control over you as before.

GRATITUDE

The emotion of gratitude is unique. It has been clinically proven to reduce depression by creating a change in neurochemistry. So, it is not merely a feeling of thankfulness but rather a fast way to alter your brain chemistry, which allows you to see the world differently and be open to fresh opportunities. Energetically being grateful is a state of receiving. It's like opening the doors to love, of being receptive to the good things that are *already there* in your life. And, it *invites more* of this energy in your life. When we are grateful, we are saying to the universal energy, "Yes, I am open to receiving; my door is open." This open door in our energetic field creates a snowball effect of goodness.

Gratitude therapy has been used in clinical settings to help people that have been diagnosed with depression. Studies reveal that when gratitude practices are coupled with psychotherapy, patients experience significantly greater improvement in their lives and moods than with just psychotherapy alone. Also, maybe less obvious is that gratitude therapy results in better sleep, improves physical health, improves self-esteem, and pays a major role in overcoming PTSD. It is a powerful tool!

Generally, the gratitude practice may be done even just once a day to experience its benefits. However, when times seem really challenging, the gratitude practice is best done twice daily, once in the morning and once before bed. For the best effect, pick the same time of day to prepare a written list of ten things to be grateful for, even if they are the smallest things imaginable. Writing the list down is far more powerful than just thinking it, especially since the act of writing stimulates a different part of your brain than just thinking does.

In addition to writing down 10 things in your life you are grateful for, you can add onto this practice by listing 5 personal character traits you are grateful for. Acknowledging your strengths helps to create a more positive self-image and boosts your self-esteem.

Writing an evening gratitude list is very powerful, as it puts positive thoughts into your mind before you go to sleep. If you are struggling with depression, deep sadness, or loss, it is especially important to add positive emotions to boost serotonin and dopamine levels before going to sleep; so, choose what you focus on. Make sure the movies, books, and social media you watch are inspiring and foster a happy state of mind.

Commit to doing this practice for at least 21 days, since this is the least amount of days it takes your brain to form a new habit. A new habit can take anywhere from 18 days to 254 days to take hold, depending on what psychological factors may stand in the way. But with consistent effort, you will create a new neuropathway that will make it easier and easier for your mind to access the habit of perceiving the world with gratitude.

MEDITATE

Meditation itself is a mental activity. It teaches you how to be in control of your mind. It is also a way to quiet your mind and develop your skills of intuition. It is not a religious practice, but the techniques have been adopted by all religions in one way or another, including Hinduism, Buddhism, Taoism, Native

American Traditions and Christianity, referred to with varying names, such as contemplation, chanting, or entering trance states. All traditions strive to quiet the mind so the divine can be heard.

Developing a consistent morning meditation practice encompasses many benefits. For example, it brings stillness and emotional control and fosters a connection to your intuition. There are different types of meditation, and understanding what your needs are to get you where you want to go will help you pick a technique that will work best for you.

Guided meditation is excellent for beginners and will keep the mind from wandering off too far. They are also excellent for more experienced meditators when we have times where we are either extremely joyous or emotionally struggling, because it gives our mind a reprieve and something visual to do. I find that I get a lot of information from my guides during my guided meditations.

I also love what I call Visual Journey meditations. They guide you through a breathing process that brings you to a deep state of relaxation and then helps to guide you to create a calm and safe visual place. For example, you can imagine yourself at a beach, in a forest, or even by a mountain lake. Creating your safe space is only limited by your imagination and preferences. As you practice this type of meditation, your inner world will grow, and your imagination will take on a life of its own.

Mantra meditation is powerful in that it gives the mind something very specific to concentrate on. It is challenging for our minds to obsessively think about any subject while it is being occupied by saying a mantra out loud or silently. Speaking mantras out loud have the benefit of bathing the body and our energy fields in its sound vibration, which is healing and clearing. Tibetan Buddhism, for example, uses mantra meditation and visualization as a large part of the transformative process to unload negative cognitive patterns and unlock the path to self-realization.

Pranayama meditations focus on breathing. Sometimes they are paired with movement that contributes to expanding our capacity for breath. With practiced pranayama, we can begin to feel how breath is our personal bridge to the world of prana within and without, and can unlock the door to experiencing Universal Energy and Consciousness. When you slowly focus on your breath, a quality of liquid oxygen can appear and leave you feeling completely rejuvenated and exhilarated. I have found that no matter what stage I am at, that these types of meditations always serve me well. One of my favorites is simply inhale as slowly as possible and hold the breath as long as possible, and exhale as slowly as possible and hold the breath for as long as possible. I have found that doing this for 3—30 minutes has the capacity to calm my nervous system in any situation.

There are endless types of meditations. No-mind meditations are simply to sit and to let the thoughts float by. Another is a contemplative meditation where you think of one subject lightly and ponder its meaning. Another is to meditate on a feeling, perhaps gratitude or love. There are many traditions that offer time-tested methods which quickly move you to the next stage in your spiritual evolution.

For more experienced meditators, having a short, quality meditation is better than a long meditation in which your mind wanders. Think of meditation as a time to soak your mind with something positive —whether it will be a positive vision of the future, divine love, or simply gratitude. It trains your mind and strengthens the neuropathways that will bring you peace of mind and a sense of personal fulfillment.

Allow some time to meditate at least 10 minutes in the morning. Meditating for 24 minutes, one minute for each hour of the day, is also a way to frame the discipline so your mind will be more on board with the pay-off. Of course, more time is better as long as it does not create an imbalance in any other area of your life.

If you feel called to meditate before bedtime, choose a positive contemplative point in which to ponder. Doing mantras, and other meditations which stimulate your energy, will likely make your mind more active than desired. That is the opposite of what we want for a good night sleep. Sometimes, I will read a spiritually-based book before bed, and then ponder a nugget of wisdom as I drift off to sleep. This type of contemplative meditation conditions the mind to solve a puzzle on a positive thought while you are sleeping. For me, meditation is like receiving divine inspiration and energy because it clearly is one of the hidden secrets to success. The keys to the kingdom are literally within us.

Meditation is simply training your mind. When your mind is clear, and you have command of your emotional states (that does not mean repressing them), then you understand yourself and your motivations. Your mind can be your best ally or your worst enemy. Since meditation is a brain exercise that can unlock the doors to various states of expanded consciousness. Entire inner worlds become available to explore; mystical states of consciousness of bliss and peace become available, communion with infinite love and the infinite impulse of creation. Yoga itself is meant to prepare the body for meditation. And meditation can be true union with the divine energy that connects all things in the universe. It is no surprise that there are many clinically proven benefits of meditation.

- *Increases positive emotions and life satisfaction*

- *Enhances immune function*

- *Decreases pain and inflammation*

- *Decreases anxiety, stress, and depression*

- *Increases focus*

- *Increases social connection and reduces loneliness*

- *Increases empathy and compassion*

- *Generates helpfulness*

- *Increases gray matter and, therefore, improves memory*

- *Increases resilience*

PRAY

Prayer is asking for guidance from your higher power and listening. As meditation is an important part of my routine, I find that the practice of asking for guidance and developing my listening skills are equally important. Sometimes, I have struggled and wondered why I was feeling disconnected, only to realize later that I had forgotten to *pray* and *listen* to the answers that come. First creating a space of gratitude in your psyche will put your mind and energy field into a receptive state, as mentioned in the section on gratitude earlier in this book.

When I am done with my meditation, I remain seated and ask a question, waiting to see what image or answer comes to me. It helps me to visualize I am in a special and safe place, and that I am open to receiving messages however they may come. Learning how to do a visual journey meditation is a great way to create a space for receiving messages. It may take time to understand how your higher self and spirit guides create the messages for you, but writing down any images you receive will help you learn to interpret images and symbols in the future, as they come. It is important to be a scientist, and ask "Oh, I wonder what this means?" Because our conscious minds sometimes place a meaning on things out of fear and miss the deeper meaning that is there to guide us.

Oftentimes, I find that the messages or symbols I received either tie in directly to the events that happen during the day or shortly in the future. However, if I don't make myself available to listen, then the universe sometimes has to shout at me through action. By creating intentional quiet and silent space in my life, I give myself a chance to hear what the universe has to say, which allows me to hand over any questions and ask for directions for the day. It is a time for listening to intuition.

I like to write down any images or insights I experience in my Spiritual Log Book while I'm allowing myself to be in this inner, sacred space. Initially, after practice, I discovered that these often small, inner "inklings" end up connecting to events that happen during the day. It allows life to become a magical experience that connects my inner and outer worlds.

Writing down any messages you receive in your Spiritual Log Book is very rewarding. It is always fun to go back in your log book and see how the messages you receive end up tying into everyday life.

It is a skill that when practiced, you find yourself having more and more magical experiences.

My morning practice serves me the best when I integrate time to (1) ask my higher power for help with my personal goals in my prayers, and (2) pray for others. Praying is asking for help with my personal goals and needs, yet it also means listening. Once a prayer has been made, then learning to listen for the answer from Divine Guidance requires skill and practice.

Our minds are super tricky and will even lure us into something called "confirmation bias" where we still see what our ego wants to think is right. Understanding our own wounds and patterns prevents that from occurring. Then we can hear what the larger Divine Wise Force is telling us will be better, giving us a more peaceful and joyous experience in life. Taking the time to learn to know yourself, your tricky mind, and how the Divine Wise Force talks to you, is a worthwhile investment in yourself. It will teach you clarity while also contribute to developing your intuition.

Another method of praying is something called "Scientific Prayer." The term was coined by the author Emmet Fox to describe a simple technique that invites the divine to intervene and solve problems. This technique "manifests" wishes and dreams so that they appear either in the best form possible or will give you something so much better that is beyond your wildest dreams. This type of prayer I have found is a powerful tool to exercise the Law of Attraction. It was also used by many spiritual people to create deeply fulfilling and magical lives, before the Law of Attraction became a mainstream spiritual practice.

Here is the simple Golden Key to solving any problem with its best possible outcome: stop thinking about the problem or difficulty and simply think of God-Source instead. You don't need to visualize your manifestation, and you don't even have to be in a good mood. You just need to surrender the problem to your concept of the Creator. And in order to "manifest" something specific, tune into God-Source, ponder an abundant and loving power that knows your heart's desires. Claim what you want with confidence. Say thank you for the accomplished goal and say thank you as if someone had given you a gift. Notice with this technique you are creating not only out of your Higher Self and personal will, but you are allowing and surrendering to a power greater than your self to intervene and deliver your heart's desire.

The Law of Attraction has its place in creating a life where your personal goals are met. However, you can only achieve results when you are in an elevated mood, and you have to take the time to visualize and focus on your results. This tool has a powerful and positive effect on our subconscious and our capacity to tap into the unconscious messages that will help us meet our goals. It is a deeply mentally focused exercise, that when done properly yields amazing results. However, sometimes we limit our dreams and manifestations because we don't allow the divine to intervene on our behalf. Also, sometimes we can get in our own way and unconsciously sabotage our best efforts, or we simply aren't in a great emotional space, and this tool then becomes something we can't use. It is heartening to know that Scientific Prayer is always available to us, no matter how we feel, no matter how good we are at visualizing and will most likely yield us better results since we are surrendering to the Divine Order for the highest good of all.

PRIME YOUR BRAIN

There have been times in my journey when I have found that no amount of prayer, meditation, or visualization was creating the results or change I was looking for. It wasn't until I was deep in my graduate studies program in social psychology that I began to understand what the problem was. I was studying goal setting and all the ways that advertising can persuade us. The problem was that it was a perceived delay due to divine timing and my own timing in achieving alignment. It became clear that sometimes the block was caused *by my own habits, by my own faulty perceptions of the world around me.*

I learned that as children and young adults our brains have a great deal of neuroplasticity. This gives us the capacity to learn new things quickly and see opportunities where others do not. As life goes on, our thought patterns become like grooves etched on an old record. They play the same patterns over and over until we consciously and subconsciously intervene. Especially if we have repeated negative experience around a specific area of our lives or deep trauma, then our brains work to protect us from trauma first, rather than interacting with what is truly there. Repatterning perception through altering our subconscious mind with therapies like hypnosis can be incredibly helpful. There is another method which also works easily that we can use on a daily basis. It is quite often used as a persuasive tool to get us to purchase products. This subtle and powerful technique is known as *repeat advertising*, which uses a psychological tool called "priming."

Our brains are much like muscles that we can train. Each time we access information in our brain, it becomes more accessible the next time the information is required to be brought to attention. It is much like forging a path in a dense forest, the more times we walk down the trail, the sooner it will become a clear path to walk on. And if the path does not get used, then it will grow over with plants and trees and be difficult to navigate. The more the path is traversed, the more it becomes the path of least resistance. It is the same way for our thoughts and perceptions. This is why the tools of visualization work well for athletes, and also help our brains be familiar with an experience before we physically act it out. This is how we can intentionally form positive habits.

Since we can use this ability to train our brains to unconsciously reach our goals, we can put this in our toolkit. Here is how it works. Start by picking a goal that you would like to achieve in the near future. For example, it can be making more money, losing weight, or writing a book. Then you must honestly examine if you have any deep-seated resistance to believing you can achieve your goal. If you do, some inner work will be required to change your belief system. In order for this process to succeed, your attitude about your ability to change must be positive. If you have the confidence to achieve your goal but just need a little help getting there, then this is the perfect tool.

Once you have picked a goal, write out a positive message. It may sound counter- intuitive, but it's important not to create statements that indicate the goal is already complete. Because if you train your brain to think you have already achieved your goal, it won't think it has anything left to help you with. Here are some examples:

I have a lot of money vs. money comes to me easily

I have finished my book, vs. I find the writing process easy

I am slim vs. I am losing weight quickly

Print out copies of these positive messages and place them strategically in places you look at every day. Some great locations are: near your computer, on your dashboard, on your mirror, or even create a screensaver or home screen for your phone. To give your mind an additional boost, pair it with something you already have a positive association with like a picture of your pets, kids, or something that makes you feel good. Pairing the new message with a positive association is using a tool called *classical conditioning.* It is the tool that is used in the Pavlov's dog experiment. The dog was given food every day once a bell had rung. Soon the dog would salivate only with the ring of the bell.

Priming your mind is using a tool that may not be well known, but along with meditation is a powerful way to condition our minds to help us achieve our goals and feel spiritually connected. We can use this same capacity to improve our lives and hack our own brains without much effort.

HOUSECLEANING

There was a quote in the great Temple of Apollo at Delphi in Greece. Historians say it was inscribed in the court where visitors awaited the words of divination and wisdom from the great priestess. The inscription said, "Man Know Thyself." In order to understand the divine, in order to surrender to its call, we need to first understand ourselves and learn what stands in the way and what character traits we already have that will aid us in our journey.

I have found that sometimes spiritual funks are brought about by getting emotionally triggered, and that has sent me into a downward spiral. Getting triggered is a completely expected human phenomenon. We need to stop thinking that getting triggered is "not spiritual." It is simply part of the journey. How we handle being triggered and what we learn from the experience is what matters. Awareness is the key to self-realization.

Understanding ourselves brings wisdom. In this wisdom, we learn humility; we learn what our strengths and weaknesses are and we understand when to ask for help. It is our task to understand ourselves enough to know what triggers us so that we don't project our wounds onto other people, leading us to assign blame and fault to others for our own overblown reactions. Reacting to people is a normal part of the human experience. It is how we handle it, and how we choose to react which will determine our quality of life. Eventually, when we understand our triggers, our emotional strengths and weaknesses, that we have the opportunity to navigate life consciously. To feel connected to God-Source, clearing out emotional debris (often called karma) will help us feel whole enough to start feeling our soul's voice, and increasing our sense of connection to the divine.

Things like repressed hurts, resentment, self-loathing, shame, and blame leave us powerless, leaving the direction of our lives inadvertently in the hands of other people. When we understand our emotional landscape, we can begin to heal. There are many ways of doing this. If you have access to any type of 12 step program, working through the twelve steps has been known to create deep spiritual awakenings in people. Also, there are many time-tested personal development programs available that have also created incredible shifts in people's lives like Landmark Education and Tony Robbins Seminars. Sometimes, working with a therapist can be helpful in understanding how to release destructive patterns and emotional wounds that may be standing in the way of your peace of mind.

Understanding your inner emotional landscape is important for understanding what your attachments and trigger points are. It will help guide you to understand how to navigate and interpret inner messages, synchronicities, and other spiritually based events as they arise. Eventually you will see that you have released emotional trigger points and are becoming healed and whole. It is a wonderful feeling!

SHOW UP

Sometimes knowing what to do next, or how to create a positive change can be puzzling. However, if you are meditating, surrendering to a higher power, practicing gratitude and cleaning house, you know something has to change. That is when the Universe begins to show very vividly that it is conspiring in your favor, but you have to be open to receiving it. All that means is to continue exactly where you are.

Accept the situations as they are but do the footwork. For example, let's say you don't like your job. Instead of simply quitting, accept the situation and use it as "spiritual practice" in acceptance, learning to see the positive in all situations, and practice an extra dose of gratitude. Doing the footwork also means to actively search for a new job, showing up for interviews, and preparing yourself to exercise a different set of skills.

The serenity prayer has been a great tool for discernment and guidance, helping me to understand when what is best for my happiness and evolution is acceptance or action.

God grant me the serenity

To accept the things I can not change

The courage to change the things I can

And the wisdom to know the difference.

Showing up in life means following through on plans, returning phone calls, and messages to the best of our ability. With the rapid pace of technology and information that comes at us each day, sometimes we have to choose where to spend our energy, but your inner compass will continue to become more and more attuned to your soul's calling as we continue along a conscious spiritual path.

Each day follow through on the things you know you are meant to be doing. This can simply mean to do the *next* right thing, which can be as simple as going to work, going to the grocery store, or simply making your own bed. Following through can even be paying your bills or answering a phone call to address an issue on which you've been procrastinating. Sometimes it is clearing up old, tied-up energy, resolving old disputes and tensions, matters that detract from your attention in the present moment. One example from my experience is that I came upon a book I not returned to the library after ten years. This used to cross my mind at least once a week, and I would feel guilty about it. It ended up occupying my mind, over and over again. Finally, after another few years, I took the simple action of dusting it off my bookshelf and returned it to the library. It no longer occupied space in my mind that was associated with guilt. It was a very simple action, that seemed insignificant. But it was one less looming source of negativity. Closing these types of loops, frees your mind to be occupied with more positive and productive thoughts.

Showing up can also mean taking actions based on my intuition. It means I am learning to trust the slight inner promptings. For example, when I tune into my intuition, it can range from doing things like working on a creative project or calling a friend that I have an inkling could use my help. I find that if I follow my gut and remain emotionally unattached, my intuition is 99 percent correct. The creative project I decided to work on may end up being a timely inspiration for a larger project, or my friend may have urgently needed an encouraging conversation. Logging the successes of following your intuition in your Spiritual Log Book will give you confidence and expand this capacity even further over time.

No matter how I'm feeling, I can at least find one thing I know that I am meant to be doing that would make me feel stronger and more accomplished, thereby honoring my desire to expand my spiritual connection. You know in your gut what doing the next right thing is. Your body will feel more at peace, even if your mind is uncomfortable and arguing. Being on your path and showing up is how God-Source has the opportunity to intervene and meet you halfway.

CREATIVE EXPRESSION

Three is that indescribable feeling when your favorite song starts playing in the car, you crank up the stereo and sing at the top of your lungs. It is cathartic, electrifying, and exhilarating. That feeling seems to clear away any negative thoughts and has us arriving at our destination feeling deeply fulfilled. That is the magic of creativity when we balance our right and left-brain hemispheres.

Creative Expression has the capacity to rapidly advance your spiritual progress. When it is deeply aligned with your soul, it can wash away karma (and any emotional pain or unhealthy neuroses) fairly quickly. We all have keys to our soul that unlock what is a super highway of spiritual evolution, without having to do a lot of conscious psychological processing. These keys help us seemingly magically heal old traumas, emotional triggers, sadness, and can even allow us to physically heal from disease. We feel like our auras and souls are being washed by spiritual glacial water and we emerge pure and confident, without having to do endless years of therapy.

These soul resonant activities are shortcuts to happiness and being able to be grounded as well as reach our energy into the inner and outer dimensions. Some people know what those types of activities are when they are children, and some people seek to discover them as life progresses. For me, it took some time to learn that the forms of creative expression that connected with my soul include listening to music that I love, dancing, singing, and writing music. For each person, connecting with the essence of their soul is as unique as each the expression of the imprint we each hold of divine energy. You will know it is a soul resonant activity when it puts you in a flow state because you become so immersed and full of creative joy that you lose track of time.

This type of creative expression captures your inner impulse to create, and the end result is often unexpected! It is usually a bit of a disorganized and illogical process. Your intuition will kick in, and your mind will merely feel like a channel. If you paint, it might feel like someone one else is masterfully controlling your brush. If you write poetry, it might feel like an ancient sage is speaking through you. Or if you dance, you may sense the music moves you and all choreography has evaporated like whips of fog on a sunny day. Simply having a quiet mind and listening to "spiritual" music may not get you the feeling your soul craves. You may need to turn up the Dub Step, Grunge, or passionate Symphony, and transmute the energy into your own contribution of beauty to the world.

I remember the first time I felt this while I was playing the guitar and suddenly a song seemed to flow through me onto my fingertips. Then I would start to dream about the song, until it was finished.

It was a deeply fulfilling experience. Also, when I was performing fusion belly dance, and I would suddenly felt a rush of energy moving through me, and I felt I was elevating everyone's experience and vibration around me. It was only when people came up to me afterward and commented that they had felt transformed, that I believed what I was feeling. I also noticed that problems in my world seem to melt away and solutions to long-standing blocks would appear.

If you already know what types of activities provide keys to your soul, then you merely need to commit to spending time with those tools. If you are still seeking the keys to your soul, then spending some time in any creative endeavor that your find pleasurable will eventually reveal the key. Some ideas are painting, drawing, writing poetry, cooking, singing, writing music, dancing, creating an art piece, inventing culinary dishes, woodworking, sculpting, and even telling stories. Sometimes taking classes can inspire your intuition to speak to you and open the door to your soul's creative expression.

Investing just five minutes a day to an activity that makes you feel alive and connected to your soul is putting money into your spiritual bank account. You'll feel as though you are fulfilling your purpose in life and also feel at peace. However, creating new habits to ensure that you take the time to do these things can be challenging. Finding an accountability partner to stay on track can really help so that you feel even more motivated to create new habits that will serve your heart's desire.

HELP OTHERS

Helping another person gets us out of our heads. I find this to be the case—especially when I feel disconnected from Spirit—when my mind really isn't being my friend. It's as though my thoughts find a path of negativity, which getting out of can be truly challenging. One of the most useful quick fixes to this quandary is to help someone. Lending an ear to someone who is facing problems helps me to tap into my inner wisdom; and, being of service to people makes me feel good! Sometimes, simply helping a friend move or cleaning their kitchen will be enough to get out of any funk.

In helping others, we tap into wisdom and knowledge we did not even know we had to give away. Also, it helps us see ourselves more clearly, and the gifts we have for others. We are hardwired to be altruistic and going with the flow of our natural design leaves us feeling personally fulfilled with waves of dopamine, serotonin, and oxytocin gracing our neurochemistry.

And don't let the meme of "you can't love others until you love yourself" get in your way of helping others. You may need to spend time to understand your trigger points, strengths, and weaknesses in order to have mature relationships, but your presence alone is worthy of love and giving love. The truth is that sometimes you find love for yourself through loving others.

Put helping others into action, by finding someone in need of support. Help someone carry their groceries to their car, call a friend who you know needs someone to listen, or even do small acts of kindness for which no one will ever give you credit. These acts of kindness will stop the cycles in your head and get you back in touch with *yourself.*

CHAPTER FOUR

Discipline and the Badass Spiritual Warrior

OFTENTIMES, THE ONLY thing that stands in our way of spiritual reconnection is discipline. Discipline is the character trait that puts the badass in front of being a spiritual warrior. I find in times of a spiritual ebb, that exercising discipline is the most difficult challenge, as my mind is at its best for arguing at that particular time. It is working diligently to keep me safe and fearless so that the fight or flight reaction is easily activated. My mind and body are telling me that I need all of my resources just to keep me alive, when the truth is that my spirit is calling me to sit still and change gears. Therefore, I offer you the magical list that has gotten me back on track countless times, over and over again.

Use this Daily Checklist, and tailor it to how it works best for you. Follow this checklist diligently for seven days, as if your life depends on it because in some ways, your life *does* depend on it. I guarantee you will start to feel the results. When you're spiritually connected and feel a sense of peace, your entire nervous system and brain chemistry will change, and your chances of staying healthy and making better choices will increase dramatically.

Becoming a Badass Spiritual Warrior is a full-time endeavor. It requires a great deal of attention, time, commitment, and focus, to stay spiritually fit. But the good news is that the more we travel on this path, the easier it will get. What used to seem challenging will soon simply be a habit we barely think about. And the reward is an infinite source of joy, union, and knowledge.

APPENDIX

The Daily Checklist

∞ Journal Entries in Spiritual Log Book

∞ Honor your Body

∞ "Turn It Over" to a Higher Power

∞ Gratitude

∞ Meditate

∞ Pray

∞ Prime Your Brain

∞ Housecleaning

∞ Show Up

∞ Creative Expression

∞ Help Others

ABOUT THE AUTHOR

THROUGH HER EARLY experiences in nature and a beautifully vivid dream world, Corinne Lebrun developed an intense love of the divine as a very young child. At the age of 8, she began exploring the world through poetry and later deepened her understanding of the spiritual with the guidance of teachers, world-travel to sacred places, and experiencing ever-expanding states of Kundalini. Corinne holds a Master's Degree in Psychology and has an academic background in theoretical physics, anthropology, transpersonal psychology, metaphysics, religion, and social psychology. Through her training and life experience with the sacred, she is able to bridge the world of the unseen, but ever-present, magical with the everyday through her teachings about connection and the soul. Corinne serves on the Board of the *Emerging Sciences Foundation*, was featured in the film **Awakening The Goddess**, a documentary on Kundalini Awakenings, and currently works as a holistic business consultant.

Made in the USA
Columbia, SC
14 March 2019